DEMCO

ALL ABOARD AMERICA

Statue Of Liberty

A Buddy Book
by
Julie Murray

ABDO
Publishing Company

VISIT US AT

www.abdopub.com

Published by Buddy Books, an imprint of ABDO Publishing Company, 4940 Viking Drive, Edina, Minnesota 55435. Copyright © 2003 by Abdo Consulting Group, Inc. International copyrights reserved in all countries. No part of this book may be reproduced in any form without written permission from the publisher.

Printed in the United States.

Edited by: Christy DeVillier
Contributing Editors: Matt Ray, Michael P. Goecke
Graphic Design: Deborah Coldiron
Image Research: Deborah Coldiron
Cover Photograph: Photospin
Interior Photographs: Eyewire, Library of Congress, Photodisc, Photospin

Library of Congress Cataloging-in-Publication Data

Murray, Julie, 1969-
    Statue of Liberty / Julie Murray.
        p. cm. — (All aboard America)
    Includes bibliographical references and index.
    Summary: Discusses the construction, history, and current status of the New York monument to freedom that was originally called "Liberty Enlightening the World."
    ISBN 1-57765-669-5
        1. Statue of Liberty National Monument (N.Y. and N.J.)—Juvenile literature. 2. Statue of Liberty (New York, N.Y.)—Juvenile literature. 3. New York (N.Y.)—Buildings, structures, etc.—Juvenile literature.
[1. Statue of Liberty (New York, N.Y.) 2. National monuments. 3. New York (N.Y.)—Buildings, structures, etc.] I. Title.

F128.64.L6 M87 2002
974.7'1—dc21

                                                                        2001055219

Table Of Contents

The Statue of Liberty stands on Liberty Island in New York Harbor. This national **monument** stands for freedom. Some people call the Statue of Liberty "Lady Liberty."

The Statue of Liberty is one of the tallest statues in the world. The statue, with its **pedestal**, is 305 feet (93 m) tall.

Statue of Liberty
(STACH-oo uv LIB-er-tee)

The Statue of Liberty was a gift from France. It was Edouard de Laboulaye's idea. Laboulaye lived in France. He respected America's **independence**.

In 1865, Laboulaye asked a **sculptor** to build a statue for America. The sculptor was Frederic Auguste Bartholdi. Bartholdi said yes.

Frederic Auguste Bartholdi designed the Statue of Liberty.

In 1871, Bartholdi went to the United States. He looked for the perfect place to put the statue. He chose an island in New York Harbor. Back then, this island was called Bedloe's Island.

Bedloe's Island had an old fort called Fort Wood. Fort Wood's walls line up to form a star. Bartholdi wanted the statue to stand inside the star-shaped fort.

The Statue of Liberty stands inside Fort Wood.

Today, Bedloe's Island is called Liberty Island.

CHAPTER 4

Building Lady Liberty

The Statue of Liberty's outside shell is made of 300 parts. Workers built each part out of wood. Then, they hammered copper sheets inside the wooden pieces. About 31 tons (28 t) of copper make up the Statue of Liberty's outside shell.

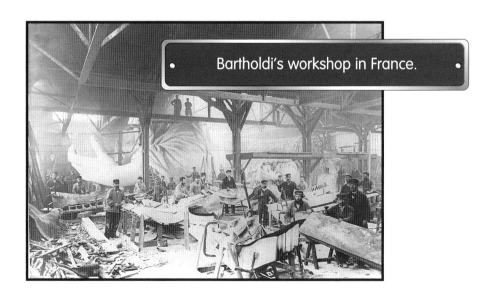

Bartholdi's workshop in France.

Building the Statue of Liberty.

Alexandre-Gustave Eiffel worked on the Statue of Liberty, too. He built a special iron frame to hold up the statue's copper shell. Years later, Eiffel built the famous Eiffel Tower of Paris, France.

The Statue of Liberty was too heavy for the ground. The United States needed to build a **pedestal** for the statue.

Joseph Pulitzer helped to raise money for a pedestal. Pulitzer owned a newspaper called the *New York World*. Pulitzer asked his readers to send money for a pedestal. In return, he would print their names in his newspaper. Pulitzer raised over $100,000.

Detour

Fun Facts

- ✔ Richard M. Hunt designed the Statue of Liberty's pedestal.

- ✔ Over 120,000 people gave money to build the pedestal.

- ✔ The pedestal is 89 feet (27 m) tall.

- ✔ The stone used in the pedestal came from Connecticut.

The Statue of Liberty was finished in 1884. France shipped the statue in 214 crates. It arrived in America on June 15, 1885.

It took more than a year to put it together. Finally, on October 28, 1886, America proudly presented the Statue of Liberty. President Grover Cleveland gave a speech at the celebration. More than one million people were there to honor Lady Liberty.

Americans first saw the finished Statue of Liberty in 1886.

President Grover Cleveland

Bartholdi's name for Lady Liberty was "Liberty Enlightening the World."

The Statue of Liberty looks like a woman in a long gown. Lady Liberty holds a torch high in the air. She also holds a tablet showing July 4, 1776. This is the day American leaders signed the Declaration of **Independence**.

The Statue of Liberty's torch.

The Statue of Liberty's tablet.

There are 25 windows in Lady Liberty's crown.

Lady Liberty wears a crown that has seven spikes. The seven spikes stand for the world's seven **continents** and seven seas.

There are broken chains around Lady Liberty's feet. These broken chains stand for America's freedom from Great Britain.

Detour ⬇

Did You Know?
On a windy day, the
Statue of Liberty
sways as much
as three inches
(eight cm).

By 1984, the Statue of Liberty needed repairs. It took two years to fix the statue. Workers built a new torch for Lady Liberty. They also put an elevator inside the statue for visitors to use.

October 28, 1986, was the Statue of Liberty's 100th birthday. Millions of people visit this famous statue every year.

Americans honored Lady Liberty's 100th birthday in 1986.

Important Words

continents (KON-ti-nunt) the seven largest land masses on earth.

independence (IN-deh-PEN-dunts) freedom.

monument (MON-yoo-munt) something built to remind people of something or someone special.

pedestal (PED-us-tul) the base for a statue.

sculptor (SKULP-ter) an artist who uses stone, wood, metal, or other materials to form something.

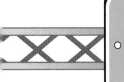

Web Sites

Would you like to learn more about the Statue of Liberty?

Please visit ABDO Publishing Company on the information superhighway to find web site links about the Statue of Liberty. These links are routinely monitored and updated to provide the most current information available.

www.abdopub.com

Index